Pothole Perambulation

Clare Conger

BookLeaf Publishing

Presentation by *BookLeaf Publishing*

Web: www.bookleafpub.com

E-mail: info@bookleafpub.com

ISBN: 9789357617475

First edition 2022

I dedicate this to all of the writers, artists, and musicians carving small chunks out of their day to find their voice and create.

ACKNOWLEDGEMENT

Special thanks to my Family for all of their support, to my friends for their understanding, and the dogs for their unwavering love and always being up for a bit of a perambulation no matter the weather !

PREFACE

Walking is a kind of meditation for me, it calms soothes, and reminds me to be present. This book is a distillation of those moments. I've sailed, hiked, biked and walked and by far a gentle perambulation is my favorite way to travel.

It is also the only word for walk I can use around my dogs that doesn't completely set them off on to a frenzy.

I hope you enjoy

Crystal

Crystal
drops on coat of night,
darker folds hide from sight,
a quiet lady in pale moonlight

Welcome

Empty
dark hollow night
cold wind shatters firelight
in the depths deep despair
home hearth sparks flair

Wake

Ocean water blue
white seagull loud wings, loud cry
treading on the clam sea shore

Gloaming

wind breeze salty air
a child swings alone
sun streams gently fade

Solstice

soft grass open field
the small children run and play
shortly after dawn

Break

solstice is breaking
the milky light of dawn
spills over the hill

Homecoming

the sound of forest
as I am welcomed back home
her green light surrounds me

Morning Dew

In pale moon light
a figure glides through to cold chill air
in pale moonlight
a figure glides through the night
she silently above the mist
has now every tree branch kisses
in pale moon light

Phantom

The phantom in the shadow
the faceless man at dusk
as the dark encircles do past, and future touch?
The phantom in the shadow the faceless man at
dusk
as the dark encircles me
The words I hear, are trust us...

Griffin

A griffin flys above my head
a song of dark and light is shed
a world of aging power grows
and the future truths are all but known
a world of aging power grows
and the future truths are all but known
in stories, fabled, told, and true
an image will be seen by few
the crystal of a griffins heart
its fearsome wings tear night apart
above my head
beyond my soul
the image of a griffin whole

Autumns Song

The crackle of dry leaves echoes in my ears
as I walk through the empty forest
its light,
the forests harsh golden light falling,
through the now bare tree branches,
on to my weighted shoulders,
it is now the sleeping forest,
that I walk through,
its spirits
abandon their places for the winter,
flying quickly and without sound,
toward the setting sun,
now all the forest folds on to itself,
and sleeps,
not to wake again,
until with melting snow,
the spirits do return.

The Novel

The Novel
Settling in to my covers
I return to my reading,
the heavy leather bound novel,
a comfort smelling of past fall smoke,
time passes, and with it
the pages, to turn ever faster.
And the adventure becomes my own.
As I read on...
The forests page green light
becomes the lantern that leads me
to my final destination
His. No mine. Yes, he and I are now travelers
together.
Not side by side, but together nonetheless.
As I sit in my far distant and ever removed
room.
I can watch and at times...
Feel his emotions fluid.
Though I am not there,
and though I shall never share with him a glass
of ale,
I, like hime shall be filled with joy when he
succeeds,
or sorrow should he fail.

But the end is half again as powerful,
as when I start,
The Novel

A Childs Tree

Cool wind plays thought the gnarled branches,
and the old tree, in remembrance of youth
sways.
Light too is caught up in this dance.
And awakened is the mind of a child.
In innocence a shadow seen...
Becomes her story,
through new eyes, honey colored monkeys
make the tree their home.
Only she can tell their story,
so the others listen close.
Till they too can hear the monkeys chatter,
in the whistle of the wind.
But the leaves, yellow and the branches bare,
and the trunk a lifeless stone.
The monkeys left,
to search.
Fore a newer place a home.

Sollitude

Green moss creeping silently on to the cratered
skin of a lonely maple.
Its elongated shadow winding over the barren
hill
until its shade melds in to the shadow of the
purple mountain,
the maples only companion.
That monolithic rock shrouded in a silent haze,
Immortal watching the growth of one lone
maple,
as its sun dappled skin
is slowly consumed by climbing moss.

Winter Comes

Crisp blue shadows dancing over the rolling
while hills
the songs of Summer pass,
as Winters quiet nocturne of wind swept silence
sends
the forest into a deathly, albeit temporary
slumber.
Now filled with tree dreams of crystal confetti
and icicle jewels.

Morning Write

The warmth of a cool morning
silence only broken by the scratch of a pen,
and crisp turn of a page,
contentment.
The quiet strain of voices singing
brings shades of color to the silence
but the silence pervades
not oppressive, but freeing.
Freeing like a new dawn,
that has yet to be flavored with life's joys and
sorrows.
This silence a new concerto, about to begin.
The conductor, of life, Time
gently nurtures the silence
knowing this nocturne is the dark before a great
dawn.

Contentment

A figure bent over pad of paper, pen in hand
oblivious to the frigid air spilling in to the open room,
a look of concentration,
mind elsewhere,
a small smile spreads across his quiet face
green eyes riveted to his querent
now visible
black marks on a sheet of snowy parchment,
question,
query,
puzzle,
concentration broken,
his smiling eyes turn to me
a fluttered beat
break,
once more he is entranced by the querent,
and so resumes his writing
so silently watch I
his figure bent pen in hand,
over his now inked piece of parchment

Dock Time

I look to the water
I look to the sea
I look to the ocean
As her breath envelopes me
I walk to the water
I walk to the sea
I walk to the ocean
As her breath envelopes me
As I walk to look to shore

Storms Coming

It might have been the darkness
It might have been the rain
It might have been first winters storm that
brought me home again
It might have been the cold
Or the hollow echo's cry
It might have been a memory
I've forgotten by and by

Flight

A house among the ruins,
not a scratch or blot.
Standing weak and silent,
on a once beloved spot.
The sound of children playing,
echoes far away.
As the children of the long loved house,
are protected loved and brave.

Seasons

Incandescent silence
wakes the coming song
fall follows summer,
and followed is winters pall
spring following wakens
again along as all
Incandescent silence
wakes the waiting song

www.ingramcontent.com/pod-product-compliance
Lightning Source LLC
Chambersburg PA
CBHW062205160726
48282CB00027B/1011
9789357617475